Catfish Breeding

Catfish Breeding

A "Do-it-Yourself" Guide on Catfish Seed Production

Anthony Adefarakan

AQUATON KONSULTS

CONTENTS

INTRODUCTION

THE HATCHERY STRUCTURE

THE BREEDING PROCESS

FISH BREEDING CALCULATIONS

REQUIRED LEVELS OF IMPORTANT WATER PARAMETERS

ABOUT THE AUTHOR

A NOTE FROM EL-ADONAI: THE CHAIRMAN OF AQUATON KONSULTS

Dear Reader,

You are highly favoured and enviably blessed to have a copy of this book in your hands at this moment, because all you will read therein are products of My inspiration.

As far back as Genesis 1:20-22, on the fifth day of My creation work, I commanded the waters to bring forth fishes of every kind, and they all came to being at My command.

And because they came at My command, all their activities – feeding, breathing, swimming, reproduction, growth etc – are regulated by Me. As their Creator, I determine which one survives or not, which one grows well or not among other outcomes of their existence (Ps. 115:3).

I am so interested in fishes, and I demonstrated this in the ministry of My Son – Jesus Christ – when He was with you on earth. For instance;

1. In Matt. 4:18-22, the first disciples I chose for Him were fishermen (fish dealers).
2. In John 6:5-13, He fed the 5,000 with five loaves of bread and two fishes.
3. In Matt 15:32-38, He fed the 4,000 with seven loaves of bread and few little fishes.
4. In Matt 17:24-27, I sent Him money through a fish to pay His tax.

5. In John 21:5-6, He gave His disciples abundant harvest of fishes.
6. In John 21:9-13, He cooked fish for His disciples to eat.
7. In Matt. 4:19, He termed soul winning as "fishing for men's souls".
8. In Luke 5:1-11, He filled Peter's net with fishes until his boat began to sink.

It therefore implies that for you to succeed in this your fisheries project, you really need the help of My Son - **Jesus Christ** – who knows so much about fishes. I will recommend you accept His Lordship over your life and the project so that He can show you the way to succeed. Remember, "Without Him, you can do nothing" (John 15:5). Tell Him these if you want Him to help you: *"Dear Lord Jesus, I give my life to you as my Lord and Savior so that you will help me. Lord Jesus, I dedicate my spirit, soul, body and this fisheries project to you; help me and guide me. Thank you for saving me. Now, my success is guaranteed in Jesus' Name. Amen".*

Congratulations! Now go ahead, read the manual and apply the principles written therein, your success is guaranteed. All the best!

With love from:
El - Adonai
Chairman, Aquaton Konsults

INTRODUCTION

Aquaculture, often referred to as fish farming has received much public awareness globally in recent times, thus the interest of lots of Entrepreneurs in the venture has increased tremendously. Locals and foreigners alike either in the oil and gas industries, banking or civil services are planning on how to establish successful fish farms. In addition to this, government policies around the world are friendly to the business, making it a worthwhile venture.

However, there are various challenges facing the fish farmer, part of which is procuring good and viable fish seeds. Many farmers have in times past fallen victim of procuring bad fish seeds, leading to failure as they either died or refused to grow. This could be attributed to bad parent stocks, poor water management, poor stocking density, poor feeding etc. on the producers' part except for those from farms with credibility which perform well and grow to good sizes.

In solving this problem once and for all, it is necessary for fish farmers to start producing their own fish seeds (with all the needed care) for effective production, and this is what this handbook offers. It is written in such a way that the farmer who is interested in hatching their own fishes can do so without necessarily being monitored or supervised, the reason for the name "Do-It-Yourself" guide. The pictures used are deliberately included for easy perception of the whole process. With this guide at your disposal, you are fully armed for catfish seed production.

THE HATCHERY STRUCTURE

The hatchery is the place where breeding takes place. It is usually indoors so as to protect the fries from predators and sudden weather changes. The fingerlings tanks should be small and have efficient water inlet and outlet facilities. The hatchery could use static, flow through or recirculatory water system.

The materials needed in the hatchery are: Broodstock holding tanks, broodstock holding bowls, broodstocks (male and female), hand towels, kitchen knife, scissors or blade, stripping bowls, 0.9% saline solution, hormone (ovaprim or pituitary), needle and syringe, pH meter, environmental thermometer, incubation troughs (which can be wooden vats, plastic tanks, etc), substrate (net tray or kakaban basket), torchlight, live food (zooplankton) or processed food like shell free artemia, various grades of feed (0.2mm, 0.3 – 0.5mm, 0.5 – 0.8mm etc) well aerated water, tissue paper and of course standby personnel.

Hatchery operation is a delicate venture which must be handled carefully hence mistakes must be avoided as much as possible. The hatchery building is usually built in such a way that the sides are covered with black tarpaulin or leather so as to maintain an optimum temperature in the hatchery.

THE BREEDING PROCESS

This will be analyzed in steps for easy understanding;

Step 1: Broodstock Selection
Catfish gets sexually mature from six months. But parent stocks (broodstocks to be used for breeding) are usually set aside for at least a year to ensure proper development of the egg and milk.
Selection of female broodstock for spawning starts with identifying a gravid fish, (gravid is like saying a "pregnant" fish). These are to be watched out for in selecting the gravid females:

1. Soft and protruded belly;
2. Release of brownish green eggs when the eggs are gently pressed out of the fish's belly.
3. Round shape of the genital opening.
4. Reddish colour of the fish's vent

These, when observed point to the fact that the female broodstock is mature enough to be used. It is however worthy of note that though different species of catfish have their eggs in varying shades of colour green indicating maturity, the typical local catfish have deep brown eggs when mature.
On the other hand, to select a mature male broodstock, you check for these;

1. Longer or extended papillae (genital)
2. Reddish spot at the tip of the papillae
3. Slimmer outline unlike the females with protruded bellies

4. Milky coloured milt from the testes removed when cut open.

These when observed indicate that the male should have a good milt and therefore can be used for the breeding exercise. (A milky coloured milt is what usually indicates maturity in males).

After selecting the broodstocks based on these observations, they are to be kept in separate broodstock holding bowls so as to acclimatize them for the breeding purpose.

It is to be noted however that it is only good broodstocks that can produce good fish seeds, hence, the source of procurement is, to be carefully considered. Make enquiries so as not to fall into buying bad broodstocks. For instance, in Nigeria, Aquaton Konsults Nig. Company is known for supplying viable broodstocks, so you can get from such firms as this.

Step 2: Induced Artificial Breeding (Hypophysation)

Before this is properly explained, it is necessary to state that spawning is of two types in catfish, i.e the pairing and the stripping (hypophysation) methods. In the pairing method, both the male and female fish are injected with an hormone and are paired up in a tank of water. After about 1 –12 hours the male fertilizes the eggs as the female lays them. This method is not in common practice because a lot of eggs are not fertilized and the success rate is low. As a result of this, we shall be considering the other method, which is in common practice and has good results. Here, the selected female broodstocks are to be weighed on a scale and then injected according to the weight. In practice, the hormone can be ovaprim or pituitary; but in this case, the fishes are to be injected with ovaprim hormone (which usually comes in a 10ml bottle) at a dosage of 0.5ml/kg of fish. As the weights vary, the dosages are to be adjusted.

For instance,
1kg of fish will take 0.5ml of ovaprim hormone
1.5kg of fish will take 0.75ml of ovaprim hormone
2kg of fish will take 1.0ml of ovaprim hormone
2.5kg of fish will take 1.25ml of ovaprim hormone and so on.

There are two ways by which the fishes can be injected, either intramuscularly (made just above the lateral line towards the head region) or intraperitoneally (made towards the tail region), but both have been proven to be effective and as a result yield successful results.

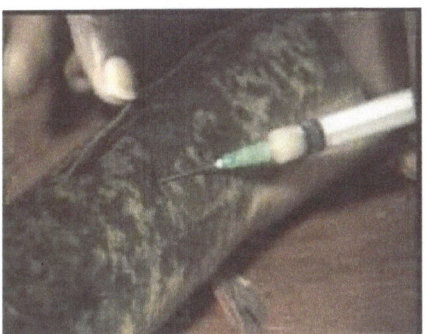

Figure 1: Intramuscular injection position (just above the lateral line)

The injection can be done early in the morning (6 – 7am) or late in the evening (9 – 10pm) so as to make room for the latency period (the waiting period from when the hormone is administered to when eggs are ready for stripping) which is usually 9 – 10 hours (although, this is dependent on the temperature of the water in which the fish is kept). For instance, at 28^0c, it will take about 10 hours, while at 25^0c, it will take about 12 hours. The end of the latency period however is indicted by eggs flowing gradually out of the fish without any pressure. At this stage, the fish should be gently removed from the water to prevent waste of eggs.

It is to be noted that during injection, a new syringe is used and the fish's skin is wet for proper penetration and prevention of injury on the fish. The injected point is also to be rubbed gently to prevent the back flow of the hormone as well as reducing the pain on the fish. The injected fish is then carefully returned to the holding bowl, which should be covered with heavy materials (say like wood pallets, heavy planks etc) to keep it from jumping out and thus stressing or injuring itself during the latency period, as they are usually restless during this period.

Step 3: Stripping and Fertilization

After the latency period has lapsed, i.e. when the eggs have started running, the male fish is to be killed and the belly cut open (close to the heart) to get the testes as represented in Figure 2.

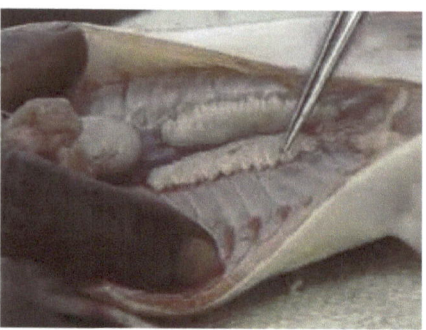

Figure 2: Removal of the male testes

The testes should be carefully brought out and the milt in it pressed into a 0.9% saline solution. The milt (sperm) should be white and milky in nature, as watery milt may not be viable for fertilization. A small bowl is to be dried with a towel and the eggs pressed out (stripped) into it. This is done by gently pressing the belly of the fish in the tail direction to allow the eggs into the bowl through its vent. Two people are needed here, the person doing the stripping holds the head with a towel while the other holds the tail with a towel for firm grip as the eggs ooze out into the dry bowl. Figure 3 explains this better.

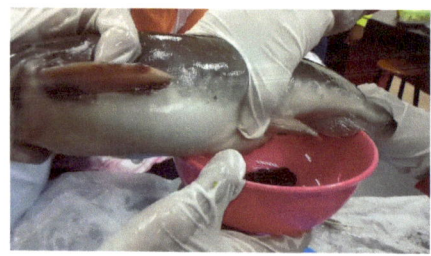

Figure 3: The Stripping Exercise

The pressing is done until there are no more eggs coming out. After this, the milt, diluted in the saline solution to increase its surface area should then be poured on the eggs by broadcasting and mixed gently with a plastic spoon or feather for even fertilization. The fertilisation, usually described as wet fertilization, takes place within about two (2) minutes of the sperm's contact with the eggs. Little water is added to the medium and decanted to get out the surface foams and testes' sacs (if added), leaving the eggs clearly visible.

Step 4: Incubation of the Eggs

This is the process of consistently supplying oxygen to the fertilized eggs until they hatch. Oxygen supply can be by means of a mechanical air pump (aerator) or by allowing fresh water to flow through the tank. The fertilized eggs are to be spread on a single layer on the substrate which can be a net tray or kakaban basket. This substrate serve as propagation beds for the fertilized eggs to become hatchlings i.e it allows an easy separation of unhatched eggs. The length of the incubation is a function of both the environmental and water temperature. Eggs hatch faster and better at higher temperatures, e.g. at 30^0c, eggs will start hatching from the 16th hour while at 23^0c, the eggs will start hatching at the 25th hour.

Step 5: Post Incubation Care

1. **Temperature:** The temperature of the water should be monitored with a thermometer so as to know when hatching is likely to commence. The aeration or water flow should be increased immediately hatching is noticed so as to sustain the very tender hatchlings. The hatchlings will start dropping from the substrate into the water within 3 hours of the commencement of hatching. After about 24 - 28 hours, from incubation time, when it is believed that all the hatchlings must have dropped off, the substrate should be carefully removed into a basin containing water to prevent the unhatched eggs from also dropping into the culture medium. The removed substrate is to be left in the basin for about 3 hours to allow for late hatching during which the late hatchlings would swim up to the water surface and then be taken back to the other ones. The aeration or water flow through should continue to ensure clear water medium; cloudy water must be avoided by all means. The sub-

strate can thereafter be washed, sun dried and properly kept for further use.

2. **Feeding:** The fries normally feed on their yolk sacs (their natural internal food) till the third day after which they will be ready to feed on external feed – zooplankton. This could be processed artemia or naturally cultured ones like daphnia, moinea etc. The fries are to be moved out of where they hatched (incubation troughs) into other tanks or vats as the case may be to avoid ammonia interference and the likelihood of infection, which can lead to mortality. They are to be well spaced out as well to encourage fast growth. As the fishes increase in size and age, they will be ready to take various grades of highly nutritional feeds to enhance their growth rate.

For instance, the Dizengoff Catfish Feed formula from hatchlings to 56 days, (8 weeks) by average weight can be of help here.

S/No	Age	Average Weight	Feed Type
1	0 – 7th day	0.025g	0.2mm or artemia
2	7 – 14th day	0.5 – 1.0g	0.2mm or artemia
3	14 – 21st day	1.0 – 1.5g	0.3 - .0.5mm
4	21 – 28th day	1.5 – 3.0g	0.3 – 0.5mm
5	28 – 35th day	3.0 – 5.0g	0.5 – 0.8mm
6	35 – 42nd day	5.0 – 9/10g	0.5 – 0.8mm
7	42 – 49th day	>10g	0.8 – 1.2mm
8	49 – 56th day	>12g	1.2 – 1.5mm

At this stage i.e. at 8 weeks old juveniles, they can be taken to the grow-out ponds where 2mm feed can be commenced for them.

The feeding regime at the hatchery (with good water aeration) should be at 3 hours interval.

3. **Cleaning of the hatchery tanks:** This is the removal of accumulated uneaten feed at the bottom of the tanks so as not to generate infections or ammonia build up and as such polluting the water which can in effect lead to mortality (the fishes being very fragile at this stage). The exercise is generally referred to as siphoning, and it is done by siphoning (bringing out) all the dirts in the tank by means of a pipette (hose) into a clean, salt free container. The dirts are to be discarded while the fishes that come out with them should be cleaned and returned to the tanks. This exercise is to be faithfully and diligently done daily for the period in which they are going to stay in the hatchery, usually 3 weeks before being moved to the nursery tanks. During these periods in the hatchery, aeration must not stop. If it is a recirculatory system, the aeration must be continuous, and if it is flow through, aeration (through the inflow of fresh water) must not cease as well. There must be consistent aeration throughout these first three weeks of their lives at the hatchery although they still need it as they grow on

4. **Removal of Shooters:** During the course of their stay in the hatchery, the fries exhibit growth differences, which may either be due to genetic variation or feeding method. Some just emerge as shooters or jumpers, being bigger than the others. And to prevent cannibalism which is an intrinsic factor in catfish, a situation whereby the bigger ones feed on the smaller ones (being carnivorous fishes), the shooters are removed as soon as they are noticed and kept separately in another tank or trough, forming a population of their own. Shooters are not to be removed once, they are to be removed as long as they are noticed until the others assume a uniform or an even growth. This issue of cannibalism should not be taken for granted as it can drastically trim down the fish population. Where there is no size difference, there will be no cannibalism.

5. **Health Care:** Proper hygiene is to be maintained in the hatchery. Just as nobody enters the theatre room or labour room and does anything he likes there, not everybody should be allowed into the hatchery room, let alone doing anything they like there. It is the "sacred place" of the whole fish production process; and neatness, orderliness, proper sanitation among other hygiene measures should be employed. The bowls and pipettes used are to be washed regularly with salt; the floor should always be kept clean and the personnel should also be conscious of proper hygiene in and out of the hatchery so as not to contaminate or bring infection into the system. In the case of the fishes, good water quality management will highly reduce the risk of infection or any disease condition. But in case of any infection or deviation from the proper health condition of the fishes or the culture medium, which can be indicated by smelling or cloudy water, hanging fishes, irregular swimming, mortality etc medication can be given to arrest the situation. Such drugs that can be used include Aquaceryl plus, Fish vit plus, Fish biotics, Keproceryl WSP, $KMnO_4$ solution etc. They should be applied at their various prescribed dosages and monitored for effective performance. However, in case of any mortality, they should be quickly removed and disposed so as to prevent any chance of spreading infection. If good management can be ensured, the chances of having diseases will be very low.

FISH BREEDING CALCULATIONS

The essence of this is to have an idea of what to expect at the end of a breeding exercise.

Hatching percentage (hatchability) can only be evaluated by mere looking i.e assumption based on observation. This is by comparing the amount of eggs hatched to those unhatched. It could be 50%, 60%, 70% etc but a higher percentage indicates a successful hatching.

It is worthy of note however that 10% of the female body weight is expected to be eggs; although it could sometimes be 15%.

Thus, for a fish of 1kg = 1,000g
10% which is 10/100 x 1000 = 100g

This means 100g of 1kg fish are eggs. But the number of eggs in 1g of fish is 500 – 700. Thus, using the least figure, we have:
500 x 1000g = 50,000 eggs (in 1kg fish)

With survival rate at 50%, we have:
50/100 x 50,000 = 25,000 eggs

That is, 25,000 eggs are expected to survive out of the whole. It therefore follows that ideally, with these percentages, one should be able to realize 25,000 viable eggs from a fish of 1kg. So in knowing how many females to use in meeting a target production, we calculate with the 25,000 eggs/1kg fish.

For instance, to produce 2 million fingerlings or juveniles; we have;
2,000,000/25,000 = 80

This means 80 females of 1kg each would be needed to produce 2 million fingerlings or juveniles.

For the males, 2 can go for 5 females. So, if x is the number of males needed,

2:5

x:80

$5x = 80 \times 2$ (by cross multiplication)

$5x = 160$

$x = 160/5$

$x = 32$

That is, 32 males with good milt with be required for the production (with all other management factors in place). It is to be noted however that as the fishes grow, the population at hatchlings may tend to be reducing due to cannibalism or any other form of mortality. So, you don't always get the complete 25,000 fingerlings or juveniles from 1kg fish, it is just to guide your production towards meeting set targets. With this information in mind you can effectively plan your breeding programme and evaluate your outcome at the end of each phase.

REQUIRED LEVELS OF IMPORTANT WATER PARAMETERS

To maintain a good water quality for a successful fish seed production, certain parameters must be checked and worked with. They are:

1. **pH** - this should be between 6.5 and 8.0 (the best range for Clarias culture)
2. **Temperature** – this should be between 27^0c – 30^0c for good production
3. **Dissolved oxygen** – this should range between 5mg/l and 8mg/l
4. **Ammonia** – 0mg/litre is expected.
5. **Nitrite** – 0.25mg/litre is acceptable.

These are just the important parameters, although they are more than these. You can either get a water quality test kit or take a sample of your water to a standard laboratory for analysis. Ensure your ranges are safe before you start breeding. Even on starting i.e. when the production process is in progress, check these parameters regularly to ensure a stabilized culture medium. With good water quality management and good feeding regime, your success is inevitable; God on your side.

For any form of enquiries
Email: aquatonkonsults@yahoo.com

ABOUT THE AUTHOR

Prince Anthony Adefarakan as he is popularly called is the M.D/CEO of Aquaton Konsults, Nigeria, West Africa. He is an experienced Fisheries Consultant with vast wealth of knowledge in matters relating to fish production. He has practically demonstrated artificial fish breeding, fish ponds construction, fish feeding, fish disease and management among other fish production techniques to a large number of farmers far and wide. In addition to training these farmers (some of which are students, retirees and investors), he has been personally involved in their business set up; providing the necessary resources to ensure their success.

At some point in his Fisheries career, he served as a Master Aquaculture Service Provider (MASP) to a Department for International Development (DFID) funded project in the Niger Delta part of Nigeria (Market Development Project in the Niger Delta). He also served as one of the USAID's Nigerian Agricultural Enterprise Curriculum (NAEC) trainers in the Niger Delta.

His impact was felt in academics as well. He was a lecturer and also the personnel appointed to handle the Fisheries section of the World Bank funded STEP-B Project of the Federal College of Education (Technical), Asaba where he had the opportunity to impact the Agriculture students of the institution with relevant aquaculture knowledge capable of making them self-reliant upon graduation. Furthermore, he has had the opportunity to serve as one of the

Fisheries Examiners and Moderators for West African Examination Council.

This book is therefore a compressed presentation of both his theoretical and field expertise. For successful Catfish seed production at all levels, this handbook is a must read.

He currently lives in Canada with his family.

www.ingramcontent.com/pod-product-compliance
Lightning Source LLC
Chambersburg PA
CBHW041217070526
44583CB00001B/16